We Generous

We Generous

Poems

Sebastian Matthews

🐔 RED HEN PRESS | *Los Angeles, California*

Book design by Mark E. Cull
Cover photo: *Louis Armstrong*, between 1954 and 1956, by Lisette Model
Copyright *The Lisette Model Foundation , Inc. (1983). Used by permission.*
Photo Credit : National Portrait Gallery, Smithsonian Institution / Art Resource, NY

ISBN-10: 1-59709-087-5
ISBN-13: 978-1-59709-087-2
Library of Congress Catalog Card Number: 2006940303

The City of Los Angeles Cultural Affairs Department and Los Angeles County Arts
Commission partially support Red Hen Press.

Published by Red Hen Press

ACKNOWLEDGEMENTS

Grateful acknowledgement is made to the editors of the following journals, in which some of these poems first appeared (often in slightly different form):

Asheville Poetry Review, "We Fall into Shapes and Breathe Deeply," "Coming to Flood," "Live at the Village Vanguard," "Louis Armstrong Performing 'I Cover the Waterfront'"; *Atlantic Monthly,* "Walking with Walter"; *Bliss,* "We Generous"; *Blue Mesa Review,* "Fall"; *Brilliant Corners,* "'like a girl saying yes'"; *Forklift, Ohio,* "Love Poem"; *Greensboro Review,* "What Love Is"; *Hanging Loose,* "Got Those Cary Grant Blues Again"; *Heartstone,* "The Surfers at the Wash, Folly Beach, South Carolina"; *New England Review,* "Coming into Lexington, Virginia"; *Nightsun,* "Taxonomy of Small Wounds in the Form of an Impromptu Map"; *North American Review,* "I Got Next"; *Peal,* "Lightkeeper"; *Poetry Miscellany,* "American Image"; *Pool,* "Undressing the Muse"; *Post Road,* "In My Dreams I've become a Great Trumpeter"; *Rivendell,* "Easter Sunday in the Catawba View Missionary Baptist Church, Old Fort, North Carolina," "Here"; *Seneca Review,* "Round the Bend"; *Sevencarmine,* "Out Behind the Barn, Bread Loaf"; *Solo,* "Ancestor," "The Night before Avery Arrives"; *Spinning Jenny,* "Wolf with You"; *The Sun,* "Green Man Walking"; *Virginia Quarterly Review,* "Buying Wine."

A recording of the author reading "Louis Armstrong Performing 'I Cover the Waterfront'" was included in a mixed-media art show, *Close Listening,* at The University of Michigan, curated by Stephanie Rowden. "Buying Wine" appears in the anthology *Blues for Bill* (Akron State University Press, 2005). It was also a featured poem on *Poetry Daily.*

"Walking with Walter" appears in *The Sorrow Psalms: A Book of 20ᵗʰ Century Elegy* (University of Iowa Press, 2006). The following poems appear on the audio poetry website Fishousepoems.org: "Ancestor," "Buying Wine," "Coming into Lexington, Virginia," "'like a girl saying yes'," "Live at the Village Vanguard," "Love Poem," "Out Behind the Barn, Bread Loaf," "Undressing the Muse" & "What Love Is." A good many of these poems first appeared, some in slightly different versions, in the chapbook *Coming to Flood* (Hollyridge Press, 2005).

I would like to thank the following people for their insight, encouragement and inspiration:

K. E. Allen, Bob Arnold, Noah Blaustein, Deborah Bogen, Sharon Bryan, Christopher Buckley, David Budbill, Elena Karina Byrne, Jonathan Carr, Richard Chess, Gary Clark, Walter Clark, Michael Collier, Billy Collins, Cathy Colman, Matthew Dickman, Patrick Donnelly, Camille Dungy, Sascha Feinstein, Keith Flynn, Ross Gay, Ted Genoways, Jennifer Grotz, Peter J. Harris, Matt Hart, Tony Hoagland, Amy Holman, Ailish Hopper, Major Jackson, Richard Jackson, Stuart Kestenbaum, Gerry LaFemina, Dorianne Laux, Jesssie Lendennie, Gary Copeland Lilley, m loncar, Sam Manhart, Matt O'Donnell, Elizabeth Powell, Glenis Redmond, Patrick Rosal, Stan Rubin, Barry Sanders, Selah Satterstrom, Heather Sellers, Elaine Sexton, Julia Shipley, Maurya Simon, Richard Tillinghast, Chase Twichell, Charter Weeks, Jackson Wheeler, Emilie White, Ian Wilson & Robley Wilson.

A big hug for all the good people at Bread Loaf Writers Conference, 7Carmine Collective, Skim Milk Farm, Vermont Studio Center and Warren Wilson College.

A knowing nod to my students at Warren Wilson College
and The Great Smokies Writing Program.

Special thanks shouted out to Lindsay Ahl, Curtis Bauer, James Hoch, Van Jordan, Dana Levin, Sarah Messer, Patrick Phillips and Ryan Walsh. You are my MFA in poetry.

A tip of the hat to Garrett Hongo.

A standing ovation to Kate Gale, Mark E. Cull and Red Hen Press.

A big kiss, of course, to my beloved Ali.
(& a pinch on Avery's cheek!)

This book is dedicated to Marie Harris,
mother and fellow poet

Contents

We Generous

Introduction

In the scene known as loft jazz, a solo performer or a duo might perform standards for an evening's entertainment—I would almost say *recital*—playing the known and familiar, but with an increased sensitivity, inventive improvisation, and a lack of the kind of extraneous ornamentation and sheer loudness bandstand and club playing might demand. In loft playing, the musician goes solo, or, at most, in occasional dialogue with a ghostly accompanist. *We Generous* is a book like that—quietly virtuosic, familiar with and celebratory of what's come before, in gentle dialogue with an evanescent accompanist, who quietly comps chords and the silky fills of tradition, father jazz to the collection's soloing son.

Sebastian Matthews is as fine a poet we might ever encounter, his music full of an informed insouciance, aloft and free.

—Garrett Hongo

we \ **1** : I and the rest of a group that includes me : you and I : you and I and another or others : I and another and others not including you.

generous \ **1** : *archaic* : HIGHBORN **2 a** : characterized by a noble or forbearing spirit : MAGNANIMOUS, KINDLY **b** : liberal in giving : openhanded **c** : marked by abundance or ample proportions : copious **d** : full flavored {~ wine}

Walking with Walter

for my father

Walter wants to know how I'm doing
so far, what I think of this and that.
It's a simple gift to be in the beam
of Walter's interest. And there's something
of the dignitary in Walter's way
with people, cross bred as it is with the absent mind
of the professor and the sure hand of the gentleman
farmer (straight out of some lesser known
Frost poem). A soul emissary, then, who
at present—as we pass up through
the burgeoning pines, along a New England
stone wall—is asking about my father,
recently dead, about how it has been
dealing with the aftermath and all
the troubled souls that end up at the door
of the dead poet's house uninvited.
He seems to understand: brother, father,
teacher—yes, even son. He's that good
at listening. And listening, too, for some echo
out of the forest, some crow flap to awaken
an answer (in me?). He just nods. We keep walking
and as we go forward, me conjuring my
love for my father, I feel some hidden part
dislodge, take wing, fly up
to join the crow in the late afternoon haze—
my body moving onward with Walter, as light
as cumulus clouds passing soundlessly over water.

I

What I prefer . . . is that undiscovered country of the nearby . . .
—John Hanson Mitchell,
Ceremonial Time

Here

What I know of this place
doesn't go far

beyond what you see here—
mountains rainy, wrapped

blue in mist—
and even that you could say

I don't know, not as if
I'd grown up here:

a rhododendron rooted
in this red earth:

moonshine stories and blue-
grass. I've grown up

in mountains like this,
sure, and walked days

on end in just such
a wood. The music I know

is *of* this place
because I play it on my stereo:

old Dylan records
with Appalachian ballads

poking through their clothes
like ragged undershirts. Jazz

is my bluegrass. Coltrane
my moonshine. If I went

to church, I'd go to his,
maybe camp out

on the blue notes
of sidewalk, let the wind

scatter my prayers
into the tornado-yellow sky.

That's where you'd find me.
And I guess you can

call that home. So what
I can tell you does come

from somewhere—not bluegrass
but high-bush blueberries,

not barbecue but
some other nourishment.

Roadside doughnuts
and strong diner coffee.

The kind of food you get
when you're going

from there to there,
and *here* is just a truck stop

and all music a song
on the jukebox.

Round the Bend

for Ali

Not all veils obscure.

Just this morning
at a familiar bend
in the road to Warren Wilson
fog fills in the valley
like milk in a bowl, only
the topmost gable
of the barn visible. We are
stunned by the abundant nothingness:
brought abruptly into ourselves
then boomeranged
back into the day
through spectator eyes.
I drop you off.
Ursula lays in a contented
heap in the backseat.
Something good on the deck.
And when I pass the farm
again, at the turn,
this time emerging
from out of a tunnel of fog,
I cast a glance over
my shoulder. Milk in a bowl?
What was I thinking?
A fierce dragon
festooned in rivers of ashen silk
roars up through the light,
consuming the barn
as flame feeds on heat.

Then again,
at the top of the hill,
about to turn onto Old Farm School,
a bed sheet luffs
in the rearview mirror.
And for a moment
I watch it float
in the sun,
a muted music
of undulation

and then I round the bend.

Ancestor

Bears have been following me around again.
I saw one the other day, across the road,

snuffling about in his Nature Center pen
up from the polluted river and in sight

of the public golf course. And just tonight
I caught this snippet of National Geographic

on television: a hunter describing how he shot
this young bear; he was crouching somewhere

in the field, face turned from the camera
as he told his story. The man spoke forthrightly

of seeing it coming, of knowing the bear
hadn't spotted him, of making a decision:

if the bear walked into his area, he'd shoot;
if he drifted off, he'd let him go his way.

He came into my view, he said, and so
raised the gun. *Then the bear turned to look*

at me and I shot him. The hunter went on,
his speech slowing, faltering. With distinct sadness

the hunter described the bullet entering the bear,
exploding inside the animal. It wasn't remorse

he choked on: he had done what he had set out
to do. No, I am sure it was recognition I saw

clouding his face. *He went down quick,* he said.
He didn't know what hit him.

Wolf with You

Life's funny
in that hat flying off
in the wind sort of way

the way dreams are funny
when they drop a wolf in
to tug at a sleeve

and all you want
is to get over the fence
and be gone;

or when the one who
first time you saw her
was the mad lady on the corner

wailing outside your father's funeral,
a sort of wolf tugging
at the sleeve of decorum,

this raving woman
with the spurned-lover eyes,
somehow the surrogate

who fills the role
the other one refrained from
when she thought she got

cut out, not willing
to take her sack of woe
and join the rest of us

in the long line
of the empty-handed;
the mad lady the one

who steps off the curb
of the inappropriate,
demonstrating the uncanny

way to get over the fence
and take the dream
wolf with you.

The Surfers at the Wash, Folly Beach, South Carolina

When I pass them again, the surfers
        have gathered out past the break,
    propped on their boards
                like the ragged line of dolphins
                    I saw the other morning,

    a school of fins arcing out
            of undulating swells.
        Then one of them paddles forward,
            rising up on the lip of wave—
            tall, wetsuited,

    a minor god flashing
            otherworldly grandeur—
                crouching and twisting,
                    cutting against the inevitability
                        of his falling.

        All week I've been
        wandering this shifting alley
            of wash and pull, heading out
    for the abandoned lighthouse
                (dog ahead, chasing birds)

hoping to walk out
        of the Self's ragged clothing
    before entering the mouth
            of marshland estuary—
                hoping to return

stripped vivid by wind.
        This winter storm, of course,
                is what has assembled the surfers
        in the wash-out. Their radios tuned
                        to perpetual alert, they shoot

adrenaline into the waves. Before:
        only a few earnest souls
                bobbing in the slack swell,
        fussing with equipment by the pier.
                        Now the narrow street embroidered

        with SUVs and retro Beach Boy
                Jeeps, all techno-color chic.
        Young men stand by idling
                cars, oblivious to cold, topless.
        The beach lays out in sections—

road to rocks, beach to wash to waves.
        The young woman moving
swiftly through her warm-up
        concludes a silent ritual
        by grabbing board and diving into spray.

The cliché about surfing
        is you become one
        with the wave—half Buddha,
                half James Dean
                        on a short board.

I don't know. Each day I'm here
        the tide erases
    its own signature
      then signs it again
            in the wind's hand.

Fall

A little circus makes its way
into any ordinary day,
slipping in with pickpocket hand.

Just today, out for a riverside
stroll, we rounded a turn
to find two goats in collars,

their sweet, alien eyes mooning
out at everything. Back home,
chasing after my unleashed dog,

I stepped into a pile of leaves
(the hidden slope beneath letting
go) and pratfell down a knoll

of blackout mulch. Coming up
in a three-point stance. Before me:
the neighbor's dog atremble,

snarling at last gasp of lead. Even
now, up at my desk, the sun
shines a spot on the bookshelf,

turning my dog-eared paperbacks
into illuminated manuscripts,
and a trapdoor opens in my head.

Easter Sunday in the Catawba View Missionary Baptist Church, Old Fort, North Carolina

Afterward Jesus appeared in a different form to two of them
while they were walking in the country.
—Mark 16:12

The pastor turns to the end of Mark,
the Old Testament's long withheld promise

of resurrection, and sets his glasses
high up on his now sweating face,

Jaron leaning out of his 12-year-old huddle
to whisper, "Here comes the long part."

He's been highlighting the service, entry
by entry, with a yellow marker, a prisoner

marking time. I am a guest here, awkward
in my Sunday best, unpressed, my pagan

green tucked neatly away. Outside, morning
fog rests lightly on the front steps,

a silent knock on the door. The semis pour
down the mountain in a stink of rubbed brakes.

We've had three songs from the choir,
small for this small church, a block

of half-hearted testifying; only Miss Fanny,
the congregation's elder, able to stir

the place with the witness of her faith.
Even that I suspect is not new—not like

fresh rain after months of drought.
I've put five dollars (borrowed)

into the basket. The place is close
to full: young families trundling in,

their children an excited murmur.
A little boy's been waving to me half

an hour, smiling back at the surprise
of my white face. The pastor has already

taken Jaron aside to tease him
for being twelve and looking pretty

in newly done-up cornrows; the old women
already pressed their leathery dry palms

into mine, fulfilling a church duty
as old as the rituals we've been enacting

with more or less enthusiasm.
Which is exactly what the pastor's been

getting at, his streetwise *I-Have-Been-
Redeemed* persona honed to a routine,

when he reads Mark: how first Mary
Magdalene then two disciples report

encountering Jesus, alive and well
and back from the dead zone, only to be

rebuked by mourners unable to rise
out of grief to witness a miracle.

They're church folk, he says, pausing
for effect. *Just like us.* He goes on

about the moral urgency pulsing
at the heart of belief (out from under

her hat, Miss Fanny pairing each call
with a responding *A-men*), dipping in

and out of song, half testimony,
half James Brown. *Church-folk*,

the pastor shouts, throwing the words
together like dice, *like you and me,*

ringing the "e" in "me" as a bell
at the back of his voice. *Do YOU believe?*

The congregation musters a lackluster
A-men. Jaron looks over, his face blank,

weighted by years he has yet to grow into.
Do you?! The two young souls, left alone

with the palpable vision, startled,
fingers laced, did they follow the bird's path

into the cloud-jammed sky? Did rain
dump down as they raced home, made

vivid in the rush of thunder? Were they
rife with the ache of coming alive

in rebirth? I've stopped listening
to the pastor, follow Jaron's daydreams

as they skip out the side-door
of desire. Have joined him in the branches

of the giant oak, gone down to the river,
am throwing hooky stones at the fish

propelling their shadows
deep into the future.

The Night before Avery Arrives

We've finally drifted off to sleep, our dreams
rabbit-running through an open field,
eager to drive down three hours to fetch you,
then back up the same stretch of highway home.

The bread bowl of neighborhood brims
with noisy dark; no one is out. Old friends
talk on the phone; our parents drift
in easy talk, old stories brought out again.

Your birth mother is out of range, dyeing
her hair in the sink of a motel room;
one of your named fathers is tossing
in his bed, signing and resigning the form.

And you? Asleep, I hope, spilled of one code,
waiting for us to come and speak the new.

II

We play the way we do because that's who we are.
—Zoot Sims

Prejudice and curiosity [are] responsible for what I have done in music.
—Miles Davis

Undressing the Muse

When Sonny Rollins walked onto that bridge
to play his saxophone to the wind
he was stepping off the stage
and into the woodshed.
It wasn't a failure of nerve, of course,
nor was it only a deepening
of his craft. He was breaking
a voice apart
and refashioning it.
He was undressing his muse.

That's what I want now:
less stage, more bridge
(the wind steady and relentless)
and room to go about
the private business of becoming—
nothing more, not a single iota less—
who I am meant to be.

Louis Armstrong Performing 'I Cover the Waterfront'

Watching, jawdropped, Louis Armstrong
sing "I Cover the Waterfront"
with his young man strut, his front man's bravado
and grace, *a one, and a two,*
entranced as he jumps into the opening chorus
like a bullfighter stepping
into a potentially beautiful disaster,
the band behind him bristling with readiness.
What is it he's got? What about the man
makes me lean forward expectantly?
Nothing flashy at first, nothing
special—only perfect time, a master's casual confidence—
not until the second chorus, that is,
and then, *stop, back up, there,*
see behind his eyes, something switches on—
he's both folding inward away from the camera
and turning on for it—
now he's utterly alive with it,
with joyous, naughty, jaunty knowing, body
animated with its force.
One hand is at his side, folded back in sassy woman pantomime,
the other pumping the down-faced horn
in frantic syncopation. His head askew,
chin thrust forward, eyes scrunched tight
then thrown open: it's like he's his own
instrument, his solo voice parading
out from behind his white teeth
in lisping spurts. Like he's conjuring
a young Billie Holiday out of thin air,
putting up some circus poster image of her
for her to burst through

years later, fully formed as Lady Day.
Like he's dreaming this world better than it ever should be.
When he's done singing, come back
from his high place, done shape-shifting,
he steps back from the mike
only to circle back—strutting again,
on the prowl, a lion, a king,
and back now, presto, horn to lips,
to one-up himself, to lay out
hard pearls of sound and bounce
through the mid-tempo number
with the slow assurance of a fakir
(he could play this shit sleepwalking)
       and out.
A big brash car, the band ticks down.
Louis steps back into his brawn,
and I fall back into my bag
of bones. What am I
going to do now?

'like a girl saying yes'

is the way Condon
put it

hearing Bix's coronet
for the first time

a mellow tone
lofted gently from the bell

of the horn

like a girl saying yes

or as Louis said
followed (no doubt)
by his cackle laugh

I'm tellin' you

those pretty notes
went right thru me

In My Dream I've Become a Great Trumpeter

"I will arise and go now, and go to Innisfree"
—W. B. Yeats

In my dream I've become a great trumpeter
with the embouchure of a young Miles
and all his cool insouciance, too.
I have a freight train in my fingers

like Little Roy Eldridge and,
without any training at all,
no real sense of the notes
beyond a school boy's grammar,

I step up to the microphone
and enter into the stream
of my solo in a snake-
charmer's trance, tight-roping

my way to the other side.
Then somehow I misplace my horn—
it was never really mine,
in perpetual hock—

and so must take up a recorder.
I can play that, too:
with its spinal cord current
at my lips, unearth

a low, chthonic pulse
for the guitarist to weave
shards of melody through.
We're in this highbrow café;

I am already its hothouse flower.
But when the connoisseurs of beauty
and taste start arguing
over history, I leave the stage.

"You clowns talk all you want.
When you're ready to
get back to the music,
you'll find me at the bar."

Train Wreck Blues

"Baby, he said, "you're a two-timer,
    I'm wise to you and the lieutenant."
—Louis Simpson

Sometimes sleep is a runaway train
barreling down the tracks.
You're behind a losing hand
in the smoking car with Black Jack Davie,
or stepping from the dancing aisle

into the red-haired beauty's private car,
pushing against her, tongue in her mouth,
fingers at her bra, loosing the latch
so her sweet pear breasts spill out
into your cupped palms.

There's a problem with the switch
or some flub pulls the emergency cord.
All of a sudden you're flat out
lying in some field, cold rock your pillow,
waking after a train wreck of dreams.

The sun beats down. A crow perches
laconically on a tree. It all starts
coming back to you: the busted flush,
the flash of a knife, the redhead
slipping out with your wallet.

What are you going to do?
You could lie there all day, nursing
your hangover, wallowing
in your beat-up body,
in the simple truth of being awake,

or you could get up and take
your sadsack self into town,
find the one café, one more
cup of coffee before you go.
Looking up each time the bell goes off

to see if the redhead's come back
to repent, or Black Jack Davie
bearing a grudge. Waiting for anybody,
anything worth rejoining the living for.
All the friends I've ever had are gone.

Live at the Village Vanguard

Near the end of Bill Evans' "Porgy (I Loves You, Porgy)"
played live at the Village Vanguard and added as an extra track
on *Waltz for Debby* (a session made famous by the death
of the trio's young bassist in a car crash) a woman laughs.
There's been background babble bubbling up the whole set.
You get used to the voices percolating at the songs' fringes,
the clink of glasses and tips of silver on hard plates. Listen
to the recording enough and you almost accept the aural clutter
as another percussive trick the drummer pulls out, like brushes
on a snare. But this woman's voice stands out for its carefree
audacity, how it broadcasts the lovely ascending stair of her happiness.
Evans has just made one of his elegant, casual flights up an octave
and rests on its landing, notes spilling from his left hand
like sunlight, before coming back down into the tune's lush
living-room of a conclusion. The laugh begins softly, subsides,
then lifts up to step over the bass line: five short bursts of pleasure
pushed out of what can only be a long lovely tan throat. Maybe
Evans smiles to himself when he hears it, leaving a little space
between the notes he's cobbled to close the song; maybe
the man she's with leans in, first to still her from the laugh
he's just coaxed from her, then to caress the cascade of her hair
that hangs, lace curtain, in the last vestiges of spotlight stippling the table.

High Wire Act, McCabe's Guitar Shop

Los Angeles, 1989

We're in line for James Blood Ulmer,
the crowd mostly white guys

like us. Seth nods knowingly, as if
he knows the night will bloom

into another dimension, the way
the kids outside Dead shows

walk around with fingers in the air
chanting *I need a miracle.*

Inside, the lean young drummer
is polyphonic like Elvin Jones.

He ignores the crowd, blasting away
in a whirlwind of kicks and strikes,

brushes and swipes. The bassist off
on an island of melody

painting watercolors *plein air,*
climbing up mountains, lost

in dark caves of pulse and groove.
Ulmer's in the corner—part Hendrix,

part Sphere Monk—laying out jagged
melodic lines, quirky guitar licks.

The crowd quiet—awkward,
reverent, abashed, cool.

Everyone patting their back
for making this scene.

The band's restless, not impressed,
happy at break to climb up

rickety stairs to the dressing room.
Another lost night. *Play out*

the next set and move on. A long hour,
and the drummer comes down

alone, starts in building a sandcastle
of rhythms, a Taj Mahal of beats

that says, "Fuck it, I'll do what I want,
you don't know what to ask for."

Then this, have to say it, this dumb
white guy stands up and starts

clapping along with, what?,
one of the drummer's rhythms?

Not even that. He's clapping inside
the music, out of time, loud

like a teenager alone in a mansion
fingering his lighter. I turn

to Seth, aghast, and he's staring, too.
The drummer furious in his hands.

Ulmer stalks the stage, tightroping
its scuffed edge, then walks right up

to this moron clapping, and plays chords
that shout "Sit down, Dumbass."

And I'm shouting in my head, "Stop it,
stop it, stop it!" But he keeps clapping.

The drum solo now calamitous cacophony.
Jumping up from the kit,

the drummer bellows through a megaphone
of hurt, flicking his sticks

not into the crowd, or at the man's head,
but into the wings. They clatter

like empty beer cans tossed down an alley.
I have been shot in the chest.

The bass player unplugs. Ulmer plays
a few choruses of "Send in the Clowns"

and puts his guitar down. Night over.

We Fall into Shapes and Breathe Deeply

A young musician asleep on a train,
already famous, or soon will be.
You strain to see, don't want to be rude.
Face open, innocent, he sleeps
like a boy, full weight on his elbows;
and though there is no way
to know this, you are sure
he has no change in his pockets—
old bandmates or devotees
picking him up at the station
to deliver him to his next meal.
You should keep moving,
not block the aisle, but you want
the light to fall like this always
in the dark rooms of trains.
To slant across the expanse
of his face, eyes closed as if
by tender fingers, mouth
slightly open. You want to place
a coin on his lips in homage
to all the music that will blossom there.

after Milt Hinton

III

What does a man say, when he doesn't want to   erupt,
but still wants to act like a man?

—A. Van Jordan,
"Notes of a Southpaw"

We Generous

Long past midnight; hard rain.
Somewhere twenty, thirty blocks

west the downtown Chicago grid,
in a neighborhood taxis don't come to

or stop in this late: in search
of the sublime, gawkers

at the *Velvet Lounge*, "soul hole"
wedged alongside *Fitzsi's Famous*,

fresh out of two epic sets—
avant-garde jazz played wildly

but seriously by a cabal of young lions
gathered round their greybeard leader—

saturated down through our jackets,
laughing about it, falling

into a kind of sadsack parody
of a gang's strut. I want to say

"a bunch of white guys," but
that's not exactly it: comrades,

then, ecstatic encounterers
of rain-slicked streets, eager

to inhabit this one particular
moment whole-souled and sad.

Picture it. Hovering there
at the outer rim of the inner circle

of regulars clustered at the bar,
we're hip enough to recognize, when

the bartender puts him on, Tatum—
his slalom runs and storm-pitch arpeggios

a kind of sped-up Bud Powell—
hip enough to order drinks wiped clean

of class, to clap in the right places,
though it ain't easy anticipating

the step-back pause inside
the baritone's circular breathing.

Chords spraying from a hockshop
horn, leg propped on the stage

like a trap-door hinge. One song
bleeds into the next, drummers

switching mid-bridge, and a flute player
sitting in, only white guy on stage,

who screams into his flute
an extended riff on the absence

of beauty. Bass pulsing triple time,
clanging like at a railroad crossing,

horns knocking together
like boxcars.

Remember that little lunch place on Franklin?
How we stepped out into that L.A. oven

to find Peter's tiny VW book-ended
by cop cars. "Bad omen," I said.

"I choose," Peter said, "to see it
as they're looking out for my best interest."

Which I assume he meant spiritually,
a black man's sarcastic prayer

against indirect malice. You read a poem
that night about being called a *nigger*

by a white man with a bar stool
for a handshake. How at great cost

you beat him into submission.
The lone black man in the audience

coming up to shake your hand.
Saying he could relate. Later, in Leimert Park,

it's me with the bull's eye
on his chest. You leaned in to remark

on vertigo, how it can overtake you
when you're out of your element.

Elvis on the lunch joint radio. You gave
me this look that dropped on the counter

heavy into the cup of your hands.
I saw you trying, but failing, to inhabit

the world in a manner akin to prayer.
Let's not forget this country has always

enjoyed its minstrel show; even better
when the blackface is invisible

and the man shimmying onstage isn't
that hit parade of soul but some country

white boy with hips like a girl's
and soulful eyes any mama'd melt for.

I kept drifting, following the birds'
choppy path through sun-gutted windows:

they seemed first to fly through a fence
then morph into schooling fish shivering

in a landscape of blue. There was this movie
you stayed up late for, ringing your mind's

backdoor bell. In it, this white collar guy
dreams he finds God crouched in a dingy closet

in a building at the heart of a city on fire—
Dresden or Los Angeles—and though He

has the head of a lion, God is scared.
The man must take his hand to reassure Him.

We catch the last train when the rain refuses
to stop playing. This kid in a Bulls jersey, no more

than fourteen, starts right in. He sneers,
"You Irish?" Then: "You white folks are crazy."

Then, with a comic's timing: "Get me
a fucking job!" There's anger there but bluff's

mostly what I see. Too tired to harass him back
or move to another seat, I merely smile.

It's a calm resignation cities bring.
The next morning the storm will sweep

through, leaving the streets wet, schoolgirls
trundling by in full dress. Beat, on our way for coffee,

hangovers pulled down like soggy hats,
we'll be accosted by a girl scout who shouts,

"You know you want it!" We laugh.
We do and we don't. Maybe

our fight is not to *be* awake—we're resurrected
all the time by fire—but to stay that way.

The familiar rocking of the subway
carrying us into the next station of night.

When did the conversation swerve
to the morning's headline slap? *Policeman*

Guns Down Unarmed Black Man.
"Same old shit," Peter muttered.

I conjured up the image of a madman
taking us out—carnival cut-outs

knocked down *blam blam blam*
with three twitchy trigger pulls.

You remarked, "Man, that's just
your white man's guilt urge

to go down in flames." You were right.
Heading back down 10 the night before

in that low-slung sports car, Coltrane
in place of the rap blasted on the way out,

I started to say, "I like my anger beautiful"
but knew it was a matter up for discussion

and so let the night's bad breath wash
me raw. The freeway crowded at midnight;

the lights of the Inland Valley sequining
the night. I thought you'd fallen asleep.

You were just taking Trane in
through your pores.

There's a story about Art Pepper.
Fresh out of jail, he's between everything—

gigs, fixes, horns. Diane arranges a gig,
not telling Art, so he wakes to the news

he's playing with Miles' rhythm section:
Philly Joe, Garland, Chambers on bass.

He's afraid, of course, hasn't touched his horn
in months, cork stuck in its neck and taped

in place. Mad at Diane. In awe.
"They've been playing with Miles. They're masters."

He'd been goofing, fixing big before.
Forgets every song in the book.

So Gentleman Red says: "I know a nice tune.
Do you know this?" And Art plays it beautiful,

chasing after the melody of "You'd Be So Nice
to Come Home to." Lets Red call the songs

rest of the way. "What should I do at the end?"
"Just do a little tag kind of thing."

And Art does. They get eight songs on tape.
After, she gives him a look that asks, "Happy?"

Yeah, he's happy. Worried, too, he's not played
well enough. And proud, bragging up his genius

like a cocky boy. The night he falls back
into dope, six months clean, he tells Diane:

"You have to know someone loves you.
When you do, everything is easier."

Mr. Rhetorical, I once asked you,
"What is it about this country

that makes it hard even to be friends?"
You could only shake your head.

Sitting in the back of Peter's car,
Marvin Gaye's "What's Going On"

on the deck, I listened to you
articulate your impatience

with our sorry state of affairs, unsure
if I was part of the solution or piling

more wood onto the fire. Memory's clumsy.
So much left out, so many subtle

add-ins. Coming out of an underpass,
I spied a billboard that, for a second,

read "We Generous"
before blinking and seeing

what the words actually said.
We've got to find a way, Marvin crooned,

to bring some loving here today.
But how? What "we"? And how generous?

There was something about that
crowded table of young musicians—

in between sets, cordoned off
by invisible rope—that haunts me.

Is it that they didn't look over once
all night? That's not it. Any circle

worth its form curls inward,
a spring about to unfurl in a snap.

It was too loud to talk, anyway.
Two brotherhoods convening

for a night. Can you even call
such proximity a meeting?

The way a man and a woman
share a smoke outside a club—

not knowing what to do
with the plentitude of loneliness

except refrain from offering
some of its sweetness to one another.

Somewhere dead center
inside the second set, I am ready

to scream, or get the hell out,
to pace the album-cover street,

wrapped in drizzle, yearning
for something to breathe my sweet

blue self back into, when David
leans in, mouth at my ear: "Why

does sabotage always answer
its own urgent question

by blowing things up?" I shout
my retort: "There is no melody

in the world worth this much
chasing." But at the last possible moment

the baritone grabs hold a funky R&B riff
and rides its steamboat current

to the night's horizon, bobbing lovingly
in its wake, taking all of us left

right along with him; and I see
the woman behind the bar

allow the rhythm carry her
into the groove of her habitual chores

as the man on his way to the john
falls easily into its rutted sway.

IV

But I needed a new way to say things: sad tired I
with its dulled violations, lyric with loss in its faculty den—
—Dana Levin, "Quelquechose"

Coming into Lexington, Virginia

If I were a drifter in town
on foot or off some old Trailways,
free of the lifelines and buoys
that attach to lives like mine,

I'd head for the bar, for
the lonely woman sword-swallowing
a shaft of 100 proof sadness—
her reflection in the mirror smiling

as if I am an angel who sees her
exactly in all her splendor, who
knows that she'll leave the man
holding her to a treaty she's not signed.

Miraculously, I have money, clean
with pressed clothes and a rich man's
smile, and I lay down bills for a room
in the town's only respectable

boarding house. And after a long
shower in which I name aloud
in the breezy room all the women
I'd ever slept with, or kissed,

I step out into the streets,
find a fancy bistro with glass tables.
At the bar: my modigliani
surrounded by cologned men

busy admiring themselves
in her company, who make room
reluctantly. Before taking her
to our table, I hold forth

on baseball, evoking the great
Sachel Page. Our meal as elegant
as wedding cake. And, while I'm at it,
this sad woman growing lovely

in aloneness, dropped hands in mine,
laughing, like at a jazz club,
drenched in joy, and the bassist
coming off a mountain-top solo.

Outside, gorgeous blue night
and neon lights spraying graffiti
on car windows. And, later, I take her
to my room, watch her navigate

the old steps. There's an old civil war
graveyard across the street we dream full
of former slaves fallen beside soldiers,
confederate and union, stones worn

smooth from the hands of bored
schoolchildren. She undresses in front of me—
dropping her cares, one piece at a time,
onto the unswept floorboards.

Got Those Cary Grant Blues Again

Even Cary Grant wanted to be Cary Grant.
We all know that. Still, ain't it hard
when the old daydream machine
breaks down on the side of the road

and you're left to change your body's tire?
A scraped-knuckles day. The pockets
of your coat eaten through by the dog
and coins scattered all down the river.

Even Cary Grant needs a vacation
from the cruise boat of his image. *Let me off,*
he hisses, as he bandy-legs the plank
and runs down the ragged Medallion. *Get me*

the hell out of here. Cough of smoke
like a balloon tied to the antenna. *And fast.*
Where do you go, though? The bazaar?
It's full of tatterdemalions and bandicoots,

downtrodden women eyeballing
your diamond links. The cafes thronged
with paperback Sartres and terrorists
who've lost track of the maps of their souls.

Gurdjieff sat there once, wallowing in secret
histories, waiting for Ouspensky
to write it down on the oragami'd napkin.
Waiter, check please. And Durell's Darley

wandered these same streets, chasing
down the ghost-steps of Justine, that sacred
whore of his colonial mind. Nothing's new.
All the trade routes have been sewn. The electric

line of college-student desire has lost
its sparkle: only a picketpocket's route
to hollowed-out monuments. Even
a trek along sacred ridgeline

no longer rings true
in high mountain air. Even Cary Grant
wanted to be free of his name.
I'm here, you shout, *I'm fucking here.*

Green Man Walking

There will always be sky days: intervals
through which we stroll, light-footed
and easy; lifetimes that fill up with cloud
expanse, then pull back the curtain
to blue, bluster and breeze—autumn
fully here, a current of winter in the air.
Then there are, too, the ground days:
those downtrodden, dark and damp spans
you trudge through, deadheaded, as if
legs were sodden logs, your head a block
of cement in the current, tree roots
pulled from the sludge at every step.
Worse, still, the empty ghost days:
numb corridor afternoons, uninhabited;
shadows and light, flimsy blind fluttering,
no one home. Trance to the store for milk
two days this side of souring. Litany of lists,
want-ads. Lost hours stalking the cage.
I want to be a Green Man walking.
To bring sky and ground with me
as I move in my life, not dragging them
behind in a storm wake, but carry
their elements within, a whole season
of life in my diurnal blood, astride the day
and in time—feet gnarled tree roots,
head frosted with turning leaves, heart
pumping out the morning's bird call, breath
a breeze after a day of deadening heat—
to come to the scarred table of the world
(avid, grateful) and share in its bounty.

Mortal

You have to center your sluggish weight somewhere
close to your hips, shuffle your feet out wide
just to stay upright, like a tap dancer miming a drunk:
the morning trek from Days Inn to conference hotel

paved with snow, sidewalk a minefield of black ice.
The coffee line spills into the noisy foyer;
you're at the end, behind a blind man's dog
who has broken ranks to sniff your pants. Sleep

clings like cigarette smoke. Later, after waves
of mesmeric bookfair babble, after the coffee's jazz
has subsided into a rainfall of snares, you slip away
to piss, anything to pry off the silken mask

covering your face. An old friend turns, snapping
shut her cell; a storm-cloud of pain bursting
forth. *My grandmother is dead.* You hold her
the best you can, your voice stale bread.

There's nothing to do but wish this dreadful day
over, thrown into reverse. No dice. You return
to your table, numb. Soon it is time for dinner,
then drinks in the smoky bar, and just when

you think everything has melted into your glass,
a man tips like a bookshelf falling into you
in dead faint. Eased to the ground, he comes to
slowly, as if from sleep. After an hour, you find him

hunched in the corner, sweating and scared,
pulse sagging, the EMTs nowhere in sight.
He's your dad, slumped over, dead at 55; he's you,
fast-forwarded into end-broken future. Done in.

Now you're lurching home to your room; it's late, cold.
You've become that sad drunk, waltzing. Clouds of steam
waft out of manhole covers. Like in a film, you pass lost
through their ghost-body. When you emerge nothing

has changed: you've got less than 1,000 steps
before your room, nine floors of elevator dead time:
the little jog of weightlessness, the key in the door,
green light blinking. Then bed, lights out. You're asleep

before you can moan *I'm drunk*. There's a message
on the phone. Its red voice pulsing in the dark. *Wake. Wake.*

Some Light

After ten days of rain, the river
        swells into a child's watercolor
                depicting a river of unrecognizable rage,

or maybe it surges, a disquieting dream
        you had last night that somehow feels
                like tremendous loss overflowing

its rutted course, swamping pastoral banks
        to make a canal in the neighbor's yard
                for the ducks to sleep in, bills tucked

into their shaking back feathers.
        A solitary man finds an iron rod
                pretzeled into a loose knot, a harness gall,

a noose he imagines slipping before
        allowing the current to take him
                down river. A woman smiles

to herself as she gathers sticks from the eddies
        of her own river, then brings them back
                to her studio to construct nests

of memories. Crows follow her trail of fallen twigs.
        Another woman, beautifully hurt, surprised
                to find herself once again down by the river,

wishes suddenly for the rain to resume
        its dirge, for the flood to crest
                over the bridge and take her daily road

down with it. All of us drift to the thresholds
        of our windows, asking in our mute way
                for the sky to relent, for a huge seam

to crack the clouds' low-slung hospital ceiling.
        On the eleventh day the sky speaks back,
                parting wet lips to sing its sun song,

and we pass down these streets, freed for a time
        to dry out our sodden thoughts.
                Somewhere down the road, a farm boy

steps into the evening's dust light,
        hands out in front in a blind man's dance,
                waltzing with his shadow before

disappearing into bright blare, the sun's last
        discus tossed straight at his hatted head,
                piercing him in the eyes, as if all he needed

was some light to see the world whole again,
        as though pain had come in the guise
                of quiet joy and exploded inside his retina.

On the Road between Toledo & Cincinnati, Late June

Somewhere dead center in the day's drive
through this relentlessly flat state, the sky
darkens and fills up deepend blue,
and the word 'rain' comes to your lips
twenty seconds before the first waterballoon
droplets hit; and before you can think
or turn and say 'storm' here it comes
spilling out of its box like a load of grain.
The woman in the passenger seat
of a raggedly elegant convertible, top down,
laughs merrily, purse held over her head.
Motorcycles cluster under the awnings
of bridges, five, six, a whole family of Harleys:
Middle Americans for a brief spell
hobos, gathering around the fire
of manageable happenstance. We'll all
make it through. No twister coming to life
out of the yellowing swirl. No pile-up crash
in our cards. The rain subsiding, wipers
knocked back to intermittent, you drive on
through the burgeoning heat: crows
congregating in the backyards of trees,
fireworks stockpiling in the beds of pickups,
young girls towed behind speedboats
in inner tubes, shouting to each other
as they pass over the rotting corpse
of a deer that, a year-rounder told,
finally fell after a long winter
through the melting ice and settled
uneasily on the lake bottom.

American Image

I want to be Walker Evans
or Robert Frank setting up shots

in the street—renegades
in Brooks Brothers suits

with Leicas draped on their chests
snapping shots of the downtrodden,

of churches, bits of billboard, bored
debutantes at posh parties

you'd have to fast-talk your way into;
or aboard an ocean liner, itching

to disembark; down in the boiler room
waiting for the foreman to look away

so you can frame his profile
with an arabesque of pipes

and release valves. I'd want to be out
on assignment taking far fewer rolls

than I'm being paid for, down
south alongside sharecroppers

and the sunburnt poor—trying to steal
moments, not souls, to find the past

inside the present, catch the already
falling out of fashion.

Love Poem

Sitting outside the Little Theatre this morning, listening
        to a lecture on poetic tone—how a poem is a small
skirmish of voices and inflections that play and resolve,
        fight and stand bristling, all inside the poem, all talking,
like yesterday's cocktail party, field and river behind
        in muted counterpoint to the babble of our bodies—
my senses bring my attention to the trees, woken by a shudder
        of breeze (blanket tossed over a bed), each tree
rustling in its own tuning-fork voice, one after the other.
        The way one day in New Hampshire my brother
and I, playing tennis at the end of a long row
        of university courts, got caught in a stampede of rain,
the shower washing over first one court then the next,
        darkening each surface, each empty stage. How
this round of tree song, that passes *into* then *through* me,
        seems now to enter the porous auditorium like a spirit,
touching the poet, who I saw dancing the other night
        in a sufic trance (surrounded by men and women
in couples, dancing, alone, in ragged circles), as he reminds
        us in a microphoned voice that *tone is not feeling*
but also all we know about feeling. Trucks wash by
        in a grimy hallway of rushing wind; the poet cracks
a joke that ripples through the theater, coming back
        in concentric circles of laughter. I imagine I am
ascending a staircase past sunlit rooms and bright panes,
        finally reaching the lost attic of my body, which now,
sitting in this chair, feels like pure Mind, its windows thrown
        open to the poet's words, and to the trees,
which are only broadcasting the arising desire of the mountains.
        (Now that's a line I'll revise.) Soon, he says,

the talk will be over. Soon, I will get up from this chair
       and walk out into the woods. At least in this poem,
at least for you, Beloved, I will keep walking until I've lost
       everything held in my head, and only come back
when you call me, a bell, to the next thing.

V

Everything is an event
for those who know how to tremble.
　　　　　　—Jean Follain

Out Behind the Barn, Bread Loaf

. . . until the tether breaks and I

am in the wild sweet dark . . .

—Tony Hoagland, "Social Life"

We watch him as he climbs the ladder of drunkenness
and falls off. Laughing, we help him to his feet.

"You're Assholes #1 & #2," he tells us
gleefully. "You've disappointed me greatly."

Later, in the slowly tightening clutch of revelers
out behind the barn, circled by young men

in beards and farmer caps, back on their heels,
hands around cups of beer or hitched in pants,

radiant in their casual attention, Ian rises
to the next level of the night's inebriation,

telling a story that is really a joke, a joke
that is also a story of how the stars hide,

like locusts, in the earth, only coming out
when called forth by the flute of the moon.

What got us started? A sort of verbal
connect-the-dots? Gin and tonic

sloshing in our stomachs like ship ballast?
Impromptu trio, our bodies passed notes

as we pushed off the porch, out onto
the dark lawn, away from the cocktail banter,

a dinghy plowing through safe harbor,
coming to rest at the cusp of choppy field—

that line in a lake close to shore
where the darker blue signals steep

drop into deep water. New friends,
our talk turning to Stafford and constellations.

We almost fall over aligning our heads
with the posture of Ursa Major's spine.

"We would climb the highest dune," I quote.
Matthew counters: "The world speaks

everything to us." A star on his cap. A sliver
of Lindsay's waist peeking out, pale moon,

above low-slung pants. Hands argue,
retreat to opposite pockets, seething.

Behind us, voices have coalesced
into a bonfire of talk; Camille's bawdy laugh,

a shard of fire-riddled wood caught in updraft.
Over our heads—sprawled in the grass,

unanchored, floating—the ocean floor
of stars pulses in its distant field.

I leave sometime after 1—"late,"
I am told "for a new father,"

which is just a polite way of saying
I'm getting old. I wonder

if Avery asks his mother to show
him the moon before giving in

to sleep's incessant pull; if he calls
out its name as he drops deep into the pool

of its night light. I am tired. When I step
out of the light, brushing the building's shoulder,

I catch one last glimpse of Ian
with a woman whose fierce silence

is compressed into cigarette fingers.
He's telling another story, or the same story,

arms folded over chest, a smile opening his face,
moths like stars flying out into the night.

A Note Left to the Next Group of Vacationers
Staying Here in This Rental Cabin

Ignore the wasps under the bed, lying dormant
on the sills: they're only sleeping through
the off-season lull. The cleaning crew

left them on purpose, talismanic reminder
of our own terminus. Try to forget them
as you turn out the light of your childhood

fear. Don't read the side-table literature;
it's only a siren call to your sleeping nature.
See if you can ignore the morning

chain saw buzz, a sort of prayer to industry
in the face of hurricanes to come. Drop
your cell over the fence, into the dumpster

where the workers pitch bottles day
after day. Trust me on this. It took us
all week, but we ordered the waves

into a hierarchy of pleasure, from "easy jumper"
to "Oh No!" to "I'm going under!"
Our tally taped to the outdoor shower.

Make sure to rent rusted-out bikes
from the 12-hour drunk lost in his 12 steps
who leaves notes on his door that cry

"I'm at the beach." Or trek to the edge
of the dunes where the crowds dissipate
and pass deep into the silence of your body

as it moves mutely among its ancestors.
Find the point where beach and marsh
become one, where land and water

French kiss. Birds will look at you
for wings before making way. Now
step further into the questioning day.

Lightkeeper

The rain slips into the mountains on its way to the next
townmeeting of storm. Morning a gossip of spring.

I am taking everything personally these days. The tree creaks
as I pass under it. *Why scare me like that, old friend?*

Old friends arrive from different directions. One will take over
my class, the other join me on walks. Where have you been?

Two friends are holding hands through a series of emails, talking
softly. I throw coins at their feet to catch their attention. *What about me?*

My students decide I should be removed from my post at the wheel.
I have already dived off the bow, am swimming in the hard surf, drowning.

The golf course opened to me this morning, a misty body, a peninsula
without a sound. I walked out onto it, explorer, fool—

My boy is the Marlon Brando of children. He swaggers into the scene
with insouciant bravado. *Cut,* the director yells. *Let's try that again.*

Taxonomy of Small Wounds
in the Form of an Impromptu Map

Fine coincidence coming upon "tattered" and "tawdry"
on my fingered sojourn to "taxonomy." They share

the same wingspan of open dictionary. And it is just
these topographic hands I will map, that so precisely

describe my week of inattention and haste—not so much
lived as lived through, more endured than enduring.

With hands out in front, face up, there is little story
but the morning's humdrum domestic dirge. Peanut butter

smudge, faint whiff of bottled milk, newspaper smear
left from the Times. But turn these oven mitts over,

as we do when reprimanded, caught red-handed,
inspecting ourselves for evidence of poor grooming,

and you will read the front page scandal in full:
scabbed-over cut on skinny wrist bone, knocked

on car door extricating boy from baby seat
after a run of small skirmishes; slight rasp

on left-hand knuckle from bump gathering books
while hurrying from classroom; unidentifiable bruise

and nick under ring finger, small constellation
of inattention, emblem on a little-known country's flag;

puffy scrape and gash on index finger; paper cut,
jagged reminder of the body's vulnerable flank;

floor burn on pointing finger, right hand, blooming
red, crusting over; etc. They'll all be healed

and gone by midweek. I'll have caught up on sleep,
paid bills, cleaned the house, taken my boy

to the park and spent an injury-free hour
in the sand, on the jungle gym. But this morning,

typing these words, my hands flare up in muffled song—
I have had my hands full, have been hard to handle,

all I need to do is look down at these sad flowers
to know just how hard the ragged wind has been blowing.

I Got Next

for my brother

Alerted by sneaker scuffs and shouts, clang of metal net, I drift over
to the worn court: a low-slung car has pulled up—music so loud, so
bass-laden I feel it in my ribcage. Young men pile out, clustering
near center court—some stretch, others gather under the basket,
waiting to pass back made shots, dribbling out for an open look.
A kid sidles up with a ball so worn it's a giant peach, standing quietly
at the arc, gauging if he'll be let into this men's club. A few more
warm-up jumpers then the ball gets checked: the game starting up
like a car on a cold day. I'm happy watching the bodies stream back
and forth, banter rising up like steam from open mouths. *Hey man,
I'm open!* The afternoon sun on my skin like a familiar hand. A young
hot-shot needs one to run. He looks over, not so sure about me.
An impossibly tall youth walks up, nods and mumbles "I'm in." I'm cool,
though pure verve surges in me like sap. Itching to get my hands on
the ball, to break a fast sweat. It's an old feeling—from high school
intramurals all the way back to early childhood rumbles with my brother:
playing until darkness shrinks peripheral vision down to nothing,
hands up for the ball careening. I know I should keep walking. Know
I'm out of shape, could easily get hurt. Though the game is tied at 11
I know, *I can run with these guys.* Body twitching, I feel like shouting.
Instead, pulling off sweatshirt, I say to everybody and nobody, "I got next."

Buying Wine

When we were boys, we had a choice: stay in the car or else
follow him into Wine Mart, that cavernous retail barn,

down aisle after aisle—California reds to Australian blends
to French dessert wines—past bins loaded like bat racks

with bottles, each with its own heraldic tag, its licked coat
of arms, trailing after our father as he pushed the ever-filling cart,

bent forward in concentration, one hand in mouth stroking
his unkempt mustache, the other lofting up bottles like fruit

then setting them down, weighing the store of data in his brain
against the cost, the year, the cut of meat he'd select at the butcher's:

a lamb chop, say, if this Umbrian red had enough body to marry,
to dance on its legs in the bell of the night; or some scallops maybe,

those languid hearts of the sea, a poet's dozen in a baggy,
and a pinot grigio light enough not to disturb their salty murmur.

Often, we'd stay in the car until we'd used up the radio
and our dwindling capacity to believe our father

might actually "Just be back," then break free, releasing
our seatbelts, drifting to the edges of the parking lot like horses

loosed in a field following the sun's endgame of shade; sometimes
I'd peer into the front window, breath fogging the sale signs,

catching snippets of my father's profile appearing and disappearing
behind the tall cardboard stacks. Once I slipped back into the store,

wandering the aisles, master of my own cart, loading it to bursting
for the dream party I was going to throw. But mostly, like now,

as I search for the perfect $12 bottle, I'd shuffle along, dancing bear
behind circus master, and wait for my father to pronounce, tall

in his basketball body, wine bottles like babies in his hands, "Aha!"

Coming to Flood

The fields, just the other day lost to water,
have emerged saturated in green, decked-out

in the new day, the only sign of the flood's
accidental profusion a few skewed mud tracks,

branches wedged into a fence, a propane tank
placed daintily in the fork of a tree, and I,

groggy from lack of coffee, drive into a bank
of fog, hung like a sheet, cloaking everything

but the stutter of broken yellow center line,
for a vast moment in no place, nowhere

suspended, until the fields reappear, now
a ceiling for the upside-down sky, another

kind of flood, one more border
crossing. When I first spied the river

elbowing out of its banks, brown as stew,
unruly, threatening to convert cow fields,

I wanted you beside me, unfastened.
You'd want to get close to the raging,

to undress in solidarity, throwing clothing
into the great convergence. At flood peak,

I took the dog along our normal route,
down through the green locks of the public course,

an impromptu body of muddy water
where fairway used to be. We came to the edge

of the new current, old road no longer a direction,
and sniffed at the air. The river had let drop

its dress, a tumble of rustling fabric over its banks;
those who lived at its feet were getting nervous.

When a friend had me over to her house, a retreat
perfect in its components, a living room made

for making love in, all slanting sun and throw pillows,
she joked: "We'll be airlifted out of here."

She was right, almost, for by midnight she'd fled,
and in the morning the flood, restless

neighborhood kid, had ransacked her house,
leaving signs everywhere of its ruinous company.

What Love Is

You could tell he was a Marsalis
brother, even sitting in the back:
he had that muddy river lilt

in his voice, the bristling intellect
and the irrepressible need to teach
the storied history of African-

American classical music. Jazz
was in his blood as legacy.
The *Funky Butt* was jammed, only this

back table free, whiskeys on the way.
A Basie number, Monk. The band
tight, Delfeayo's trombone aflame

from the opening chorus. I even
didn't mind that nearby tables
were more chatter than rapt attention,

or that our waitress took her time.
For Delfeayo was holding forth
on the subject of "cuttin'," that

fraternal pissing contest where raw-
boned skill and bravado run loose
to fight for the night's supremacy.

When the trumpet got introduced,
he looked over at Marsalis, a little
reticent to step into the ring.

Who could blame him? Delfeayo was all
over the bone: so low in the register
your feet could feel it; so high

he was bumping the night's rafters.
And not just range. He donned all the hats
of virtuosity in rapid succession

and swung like crazy, too. The trumpeter
was game, following behind
like a younger brother, tossing up

the bell of his horn, blatting out wild
roundhouse notes. But he was going
down. And when he managed a high

C, and held it, it came from his waist:
he'd been cut off at the legs. We
nearly jumped out of our seats, like

at some cellar cock fight.
At the break, heading for the john,
I spied a couple groping

in the dark hall; the woman pushing
the man up against a wall, kissing
him hard; his hand cupping her ass.

And when the waitress set down our drinks,
her breasts dropping like ripe peaches,
a cowgirl tattoo dancing on her arm,

I just about burst into happiness—
for being among friends,
for loving my wife, who

I knew, was at home
in front of the fire, dog asleep
at her feet—and raised a silent

toast to the night unfolding:
to soulful music and to the grace-
ful glance of good luck's passing.

Later, when Delfeayo plays
the loveliest solo on "You Don't Know
What Love Is" I ever heard

(heroin slow, each note laid out
like an early morning baker
sets out a rack of bread loaves)

the place gets church quiet, drinks
clinking as we listen in
on a one-way lover's plea

into the grimy pay phone of the blues.
Before we leave, the couple returns,
the guy's shirt back basted

with brick dust and sweat. I shake
Marsalis' hand on the way out
in that tentative way blacks and whites

do, half soul shake, half *how you do?*
and tell him what I think of his solo.
He gives me a look I can't read,

that I like to think registered surprise.
What do I know? Out on the street,
on the walk back to the hotel,

past a broken-bottled Congo Square,
the four of us picked our way
through the drunks—city still

bustling past midnight, sidewalks
slick from a streetsweep of rain—
jabbering about the prize fight

of a set, and I tried to
tell my friend something
of the feeling that had taken

hold of me, stumbling over
the words like a greenhorn
sitting in. He listened, rapt, happy,

filling in the last gap
of my music with a huge *whoop*
and then, steps later, *Wow!*

Wow! and we crossed over
onto Canal, heads bent in reverie
for all the night had offered up in its swell.

"Here" is dedicated to Van Jordan.

"Wolf with You" is dedicated to Dana Levin.

"The Surfers at the Wash, Folley Beach, South Carolina" is dedicated to Noah Blaustein.

"Easter Sunday in the Catawba View Missionary Baptist Church, Old Fort, North Carolina" is dedicated to Emilie White.

The archival footage described in "Louis Armstrong Performing 'I Cover the Waterfront'" can be viewed in Ken Burn's documentary series *Jazz*.

The dialogue in 'like a girl saying yes' comes out of Ted Gioia's *The History of Jazz* (Oxford University Press).

"Train Wreck Blues" is dedicated to Gary Clark. The last line of the poem is from the old blues/folk tune "Dehlia," covered by Bob Dylan on *World Gone Wrong*.

"High Wire Act, McCabe's Guitar Shop" is dedicated to Gary Copeland Lilley.

"We Fall into Shapes and Breathe Deeply" responds to a photographs by Milt Hinton of a young Dizzy Gilllespe. The photo appears in Hinton's excellent book, *Bass Line*.

"We Generous" is dedicated to Curtis Bauer, David Budbill, James Hoch, Patrick Rosal, Ryan Walsh & Jon Wei, who were there. The movie referenced in the poem's 4th section is *The Big Kahuna*, starring Kevin Spacey. The story in the 7th section, as well as much of its dialogue, comes out of Art Pepper's autobiography *Straight Life* (Da Capo Press).

"Green Man Walking" is dedicated to Ryan Walsh.

"Mortal" is dedicated to Jasmine Beach-Ferrara.

"Some Light" is dedicated to Sean Nevin.

"Love Poem" is dedicated to Tony Hoagland. The line quoted is his.

"Out Behind the Bar, Bread Loaf" is dedicated to Patrick Phillips. The lines quoted come from two William Stafford poems.

"A Note Left to the Next Group of Vacationers Staying Here in This Rental Cabin" is dedicated to Matthew Dickman.

"Lightkeeper" is dedicated to Sarah Messer.

"What Love Is" is dedicated to Sascha Feinstein.

1.
"Mountain Man"
Collage Using Magazine Images on a Postcard Reproducing Richard
Diebenkorn's "Ocean Park # 54"

2.
"Woodshedding at the 3 Deuces"
Collage on Top of an Old Postcard Using a Photo of Illinois Jacquet
and Other Magazine Images

3.
"Brothers"
Collage Using a French Postcard of Stan Getz & Miles Davis
with Images from Danny Lyon's *The Destruction of Lower Manhattan*

4.
"The Look"
Collage Using a Postcard of John Baldesarri's "Man & Woman with Bridge,
1984" along with Various Magazine Images and Color Fragments

5.
"Mixed Emotion"
Collage Using a Postcard of the Photograph "Billy's Roses"
by Bruce Cratsley conflated with Images from Danny Lyon's
The Destruction of Lower Manhattan

"Woodshedding at the 3 Deuces" and "Brothers" first appeared in the Jazz
Issue of the *Asheville Poetry Review* (2006)

BIOGRAPHICAL NOTE

Sebastian Matthews is the author of the memoir *In My Father's Footsteps* and co-editor, with Stanley Plumly, of *Search Party: Collected Poems of William Matthews*. Matthews lives with his wife and son in Asheville, North Carolina, where he teaches part-time at Warren Wilson College and the Great Smokies Writing Program and edits *Rivendell*, a place-based literary journal.

Printed in the USA
CPSIA information can be obtained
at www.ICGtesting.com
JSHW081123110823
46380JS00001B/1